Did you die?

A tiny tale of transience and
transformation...

J L Ayodele

DEDICATION

To every heart hiding in a human shell…

CONTENTS

Did you die?

Prologue

Everything is Everything.

Change is the only constant.

Impermanence, constant recycling, continuous motion and conversion create the miracle of being alive.

Here you are, for this moment, in the hurricane of change; Sometimes thrown around in the storm and sometimes observing the chaos from within the eye.

To die is just transformation and for that we have our whole lives to practice.

A little poem

It has been said a million times,

Yet, still, it seems so strange... -

That all we can be sure of

Is that everything will change.

Chapter 1: An apparent beginning

A Baby was born. It was very small and its skin was soft and new. The Baby was a boy, but he didn't know it yet.

On the day he was born, he received a
special gift from a mysterious old woman
with bright green eyes.

The gift was a little Turtle.

Because neither the Baby nor the Turtle could talk, they would communicate in their own special way.

One day, the Baby looked at the Turtle and saw it had disappeared. There was only a shell.

"Did you die?" The Baby asked without words.

"No, don't worry," replied the Turtle, "I'm just hiding for a while!"

Chapter 2: Seasons change

When the Baby was 5, he looked very different and had grown tiny teeth and hair. He was called a Little Boy.

The Little Boy and the Turtle grew bigger
every day.

One afternoon, they sat together on a big
round Rock under a Tree.

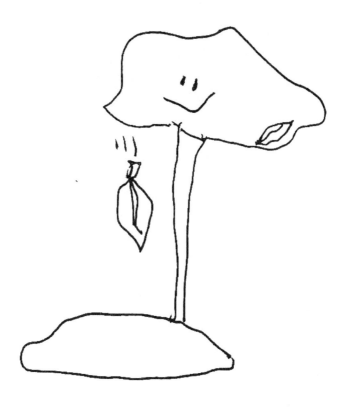

They watched a Leaf fall to the ground.

The Tree didn't look sad to lose its Leaf.

"Did you die?" The Little Boy asked the Leaf.

"No, don't worry," replied the Leaf. I'm changing. I will become the ground."

"What?" cried the Little Boy.

"Yes, the Tree lets me go and then I will meet the tree again from down here."

Chapter 3: Practice makes progress

When the Baby was 10 he had changed again. He wasn't so little any more, just Boy. He had longer legs and was wearing glasses.

One day he took the Turtle into the garden and they watched a Caterpillar wrap itself up in a chrysalis.

It was very still and serious and quiet.

"Did you die?" The Boy asked the Caterpillar.

"No, don't worry," a voice replied from the cocoon, " I am changing, soon I will be a Butterfly."

"HOW?" cried the Boy.

"First I dissolve my old-self and then I remember how to put my new-self back together again."

"The beauty of a Butterfly becomes even more incredible when you realize that after all the years of falling, the leaves finally found the joy of learning to fly." Smiled the Turtle.

Chapter 4: Simultaneously disappearing and reappearing

When the Baby was 15 he had changed yet again! He was even taller and his hair and skin were different. There were metal braces on his teeth and his new name was Teenager.

One night, he finished his writing and looked at his Pencil. It was gone! Only the wooden top remained.

"Did you die?" The Teenager asked the Pencil.

"No, don't worry," replied the Pencil, "I changed. Now I'm the words on your page."

"Oh, I'm so sorry!" Said the Teenager.

"Don't be sorry," Said the Pencil, "for I have become a beautiful Poem!"

("And just for the record," said the Paper, "I used to be a tree, but I changed too!")

Chapter 5: Breaking to become

When the Baby was 20 he was completely different and now called a Young Man.

His teeth were straight and he had to start "being responsible" and wearing very stiff suits.

A bird had built a nest in the Tree by his favourite round Rock and there were lots of Eggs inside.

One evening, the Young Man took the Turtle to see the Eggs.

But they were gone!

"Did you die?" The Young Man asked the Egg shells.

"No, don't worry, we changed! It turns out we were Birds all along!" Sang the little Chicks.

"Something else that hides in a shell…" Smiled the Turtle.

Chapter 6: The Existential Crisis

When the Baby was 25, he was an Adult and known simply as a Man. He didn't feel like an Adult, he felt complicated and confused.

One rare night, after work, he went
camping with some friends, being in
nature felt so strange.

Once everyone had gone to bed, he
stayed to watch the Fire. The flames were
hypnotizing.

Slowly, it burnt out...

"Did you die?" Asked the Man.

"No, don't worry," whispered the Fire, "I just changed and became the Wind. Every second I was many different flames turning into the Wind."

"What about all that you burn… does that die?" Wondered the Man.

"No, it travels until it finds the right place to settle and change."

The next morning, the Man gave away his stiff suit, packed the Turtle and set off travelling.

Chapter 7: The stuff we are made of

When the Baby was 30, he was hairier
and his body and mind were heavy with
experiences. He had found a wife with
bright green eyes and the happiest
laughter. His title was Mr.

One afternoon, he sat on his favourite
round Rock under the Tree and an Apple
fell beside him.

"Did you die?" Asked the Mr.

"No, don't worry," replied the Apple, "I'm changing into the ground, maybe even into another Tree."

The Turtle was hungry and took a bite of the Apple, feeling very thankful.

"Now did you die?" The Mr. asked looking worried.

"No, don't worry," Said Apple, "now I'm changing into part of your Turtle."

The Mr. sat and thought about all the food he had eaten.

Chapter 8: Sowing seeds

When the Baby was 35, he started losing some of his hair and had changed his name to Dad.

Every day he took his Daughter to pick yellow Flowers.

One morning, the yellow Flowers were gone!

In their place were fluffy white balls with seeds in the middle.

"Did you die?" Dad asked the Flowers.

"No, don't worry, we changed - Now we are wishes!" They laughed.

"If weeds can become wishes, anything is possible." Said the Turtle as they watched the Little Daughter blow them away.

Chapter 9: Cycles

When the Baby was 40, his hair started to turn white and his face was getting wrinkles, so he was called Middle-aged.

He often went back to his favourite Rock
to watch the sky.

The Clouds were growing and shrinking,
coming and going, forming, reforming.

After a while, the sky was completely
blue, all the Clouds had disappeared.

"Did you die?" Asked the Middle-aged.

"No, don't worry," replied the Clouds "we are always changing, all sorts of shapes and sizes, we never stay the same.

Ocean to droplets to cloud to rain, rain to ocean and back again."

Chapter 10: Shedding the skin

When the baby was 45, hoping that he was still Middle-aged, he looked in the mirror one morning and didn't recognize himself.

The Turtle didn't look any different, the Hopefully-still-middle-aged rolled his weary eyes, why did Humans have to change so much!?

He decided it was time for a holiday and he took his family to relax in the sun.

On a walk down the desert track, he saw a
Snake. It wasn't moving.

"Did you die?" Asked the Hopefully-still
middle-aged man.

"No, don't worry, I just changed…" a voice
hissed behind him, "That's my old, tired
skin, it didn't fit anymore, so I left it
behind." The bright green Snake whizzed
off across the sand dunes.

"Another shell…" Smiled the Turtle.

Chapter 11: Absence of light to find light

When the Baby was 50, he was feeling much better. He accepted the 50 candles on his cake and had developed different, healthier habits. Many people called him Sir.

One night he went to the round Rock and
sat under the Tree to watch the sunset.
The Sun sank in a rosy sky and
disappeared on the horizon.

"Did you die?" He asked the Sun.

"No, don't worry, I'm changing." Replied
the Sun, "I'm lighting up a different place."

"But, now it's dark here" said the Sir.

"Darkness is necessary. Or else, how
would you meet the Stars."

"The Sun always makes an important
point." The Turtle added.

Chapter 12: Letting go

When the baby was 55 he started wearing suits again, just for fun.

His body was slower and his skin was getting brown spots and different coloured marks.

It was the night of his Little Daughters' graduation ball. He and his wife watched their baby come down the stairs in a beautiful gown.

The Father didn't recognize her.

"Did you die?" He shrieked.

"No Dad, don't worry," she laughed. "I just changed into a Butterfly." She kissed him on the cheek and fluttered out into the darkness.

The Father watched with a concerned frown.

The Turtle nudged his leg, "If the Trees held onto their leaves, they would have never learned to fly."

Chapter 13: Accepting progress

When the Baby was 60 he was different still.

Some of his teeth were gone for good and his hair was almost completely white. People told him he was Getting-on-a-bit.

Most nights he would sit on the round rock to watch the night sky and think about what the Sun had told him.

Once, at midnight, he watched a star explode and completely disappear from sight.

"Did you die?" cried the Getting-on-a-bit.

"No, don't worry, I changed, I'm in a different part of space now. Maybe you'll see me again in another universe!" Echoed the Stardust from a potentially new 164^78x9^∞th Quantum dimension of the Cosmos.

The Getting-on-a-bit stared blankly at the empty piece of sky, completely confused.

"It's a generational thing, don't overthink it." Muttered the Turtle.

Chapter 14: Dust to dust

When the Baby was 65 he decided he was officially old(er).

It had been a slower process than he had once thought, it wasn't so bad.

He took a leisurely walk to sit under the tree on his favourite Rock.

To his surprise, the once round Rock was now flat and almost covered in grass.

"Did you die?" questioned the Older.

"No, don't worry I'm changing," said the
Rock, "I was worn away by all the
footsteps and rain, now I'm sand and
memories...

The Older sat on what was left of the Rock and thought about when he sat there as a child.

His body was being worn away too, and his mind was just made of memories.

"…Humans are just a bundle of memories and dreams…" he told the Turtle.

Chapter 15: Love is never lost

When the Baby was 70, he got new teeth that he could put in and take out. He liked telling bad jokes and his Wife called him Old Man.

His Wife with the bright green eyes and happiest laughter became sick.

The Old Man took the Turtle with him to stay in the hospital.

Every night, he lay next to his Love and spoke to her about their adventures, told her of the stars, the changing clouds, the dreams and happy memories in his mind.

When her chest stopped moving, the Old Man asked quietly,

"Did you die?"

"No", said a soft voice in his heart "I'm changing..."

The Old man waited in the silence. "...But, into what?" He wept at last.

"Be patient," Said the Turtle.

Chapter 16: An apparent beginning

By the time the Baby was 75, he had a
brand new name, Grandpa.

His tiny Granddaughter had bright green
eyes and a familiar happy laugh that filled
him with love and joy every day.

Life was so peaceful as he understood more with each moment the cycles of water and clouds, day and night, the growing of trees and the falling of leaves.

One glorious sunset, he walked very steadily to his favourite Rock – now flat land. He placed the Turtle down beside him and leant on the old, strong Tree.

Side by side, they watched the Sun sink and the Moon and Stars take their turn to glow in the darkness.

"Do you remember when I was a baby?" Said the Grandpa to the Turtle.

"Of course," said the Turtle.

"I changed so much," sighed the Grandpa looking at his old hands.

"Only the shell." the Turtle replied.

The Grandpa smiled with contentment, placed the Turtle in his lap and closed his eyes.

All was very quiet. Only the hum of the insects and the gentle whisper of the breeze.

The Turtle looked at the Baby and saw it had disappeared. There was only a shell.

"Did you die?" The Turtle asked without words.

"No, don't worry," Said the Baby, "I'm just hiding for a while."

Epilogue

If you can look beyond the different shapes and sizes that our bodies have grown into, if you can look beyond the identities, conditions, information and concepts that we all carry, if you can look beyond the memories and dreams that we are made of, what is left?

Hiding within each of us there is a little baby, trying to survive, wanting to be loved, maybe still believing that weeds can be wishes and wondering what on earth is going on!?

ABOUT THE AUTHOR

Image Credit - Mikhail Kalashnikov

Jennifer Louise writes books for children and children's books for adults, to share some thoughts and ideas in a simple, creative way.
Always with love, curiosity and the highest hopes for the future, J.

P.s. In the true nature of change, why not pass this book on to someone else. Maybe put a little paper note **here** for them to find at the end – share a thought or some kind words and they can do the same for another stranger or friend.

Printed in Great Britain
by Amazon